"A WAY TO ACHIEVEMENT"

"A Way To Achievement"

BY

MOTHER BOLTON
Religious of the Cenacle

In collaboration with
G. McL. H.

2020
ST. AUGUSTINE ACADEMY PRESS
HOMER GLEN, ILLINOIS

Nihil Obstat:

JOHN M. A. FEARNS, S.T.D.,
Censor Librorum.

Imprimatur:

✠ FRANCIS CARDINAL SPELLMAN,
Archbishop of New York.

New York, November 17, 1948.

This book was originally published in 1940
by The Paulist Press.

This facsimile edition reprinted in 2020
by St. Augustine Academy Press.

ISBN: 978-1-64051-111-8

"THE MYSTERY WHICH HATH BEEN
HIDDEN FROM FORMER AGES AND
GENERATIONS BUT NOW . . . HATH
BEEN MADE MANIFEST . . . CHRIST
IN YOU, YOUR HOPE OF GLORY."

(Colossians i. 26.)

INTRODUCTION

"It is the mood today to blame institutions for the chaos of the world, and to point our fingers at property, finances, parliaments and exchange, as things which have broken down and toppled civilization on our heads.

"Nothing could be further from the truth.

"It is not institutions which have failed; it is men.

"Land, money, senates, and banks have no morality in themselves, any more than a stone. Their morality comes from the way they are used by men. If men were good, banks would be good, if men were good, parliaments would be good; but if a man is bad, he can pervert even the beautiful lilies of the field.

"*We point the sword of blame at things, only because we have not the courage to run it into our own hearts.*

"The only reason we war with our neighbors is because we have refused to war with ourselves and our baser instincts; the only reason there is civil strife among men is because man has not put down the civil war in his own heart.

"The world needs a revolution now as it never needed it before—not a revolution against things, but a revolution against the heart's injustice; not violence against our neighbor's wealth, but violence against our own avarice; *not a war against something outside man, but a war against something inside, namely, his pride, his selfishness, and his own greed.*

"The restoration of the world's peace waits for a leadership which will put the blame where it belongs, namely, not on politics but on politicians, not on money-lending but on money lenders, not on an ism but on men. . . .

"As Pius XI put it: 'No leader in public life, no power of organization will ever be able to bring social conditions to a peaceful solution, until first there is made to reign the moral law based on God and conscience.' " *

---

* From an Address given by Monsignor Fulton J. Sheen, February 12, 1939.

PART I

"MY THOUGHTS ARE NOT YOUR
THOUGHTS: NOR YOUR WAYS MY
WAYS, SAITH THE LORD."

(Isaias lv. 8.)

YOU

regardless of environment, education, age or opportunities, can make your personal life rich in joy and achievement. And you can also help to bring greater happiness and opportunity to others.

This realization will come through the Grace of God in you and the applying of the teachings of Jesus to your daily life.

All of Jesus' counsels are vital, practical and workable. *But just to know them will not change your life!*

You will need to "Make trial of your own selves, whether ye be in the Faith."

You Must "Prove Your Own Selves."

(2 Cor. xiii. 5.)

BE YE TRANSFORMED

IT is common knowledge that for healthy living, it is essential to give thought to the diet of the physical being.

But it is not so generally recognized that it is even more necessary to consider what "food for thought" is being given to the mental being. For *right thinking* gives a well-balanced mental life in something the same way as right food gives a healthy physical life.

To be a happy useful person, it is necessary for you to understand the tremendous importance of your habitual thinking.

*   *   *

Should your thinking be wrong you cannot make progress because what you do will depend upon what you think.

*   *   *

If you feed your mind upon muddled, deceitful or despairing thoughts you will live a life of frustration; whereas by feeding your mind with orderly, honest, original thoughts you will be working toward a life of rich and satisfactory achievement.

For the quality of your thought, be it for strength or weakness,—be it for success or failure,—be it for good or bad,—determines your outlook upon life; *and to a great extent your outlook upon life will mean for you contentment or dissatisfaction.*

*　　*　　*

Perhaps you think that if you had some special influence, could change your work, your place of business, get married, or make some other vital change, life would be more to your liking.

But any one of these desires could be fulfilled without bringing contentment, because with the change another situation might develop causing equal dissatisfaction.

Or it may be that you desire your circumstances improved, but expect this to come about without any disturbance to your selfish interests or your love of ease. Should this be the situation, *you are looking outside of yourself for the resources you need instead of within;* not realizing that usually there must be a change of thought before the outer conditions will be altered.

In other words: *"Be ye transformed by the renewing of your mind."* (Romans xii. 2.)

* * *

Jesus, Himself, the Greatest Teacher of all times, said: "The Kingdom of God is Within You"* — meaning your mind, with its thoughts "lighted by participation in eternal Truth." **

Therefore, if your thinking is confused, it is most necessary to "renew your mind" bringing it into harmony with the teachings of Jesus.

---

* Luke xvii. 21.
** St. Augustine.

FACING YOUR THOUGHTS

TO reap the benefits of Jesus' teaching, "Be Renewed in the Spirit of Your Mind," (Eph. iv. 23) you must have the courage to face your thoughts squarely.

Do you honestly try to know your real self? Or do you, perhaps, unconsciously, so dislike blaming yourself that you give excuses for your motives instead of admitting the true facts?

And do you make an honest effort to think rightly concerning other people?

Since your thoughts help to determine your character, and your character colors your whole life, you should endeavor to hold thoughts of kindness, tolerance, forgiveness, service, Faith, Hope and Love,—that is, you must, with a spirit of patience, fortitude, honesty and good will, practice rational, constructive thinking.

For the kind person has kind thoughts; the brave person courageous thoughts; the successful person constructive thoughts; the spiritual person Christlike thoughts.

*   *   *

As you become more deeply conscious of the fact that the state of your mentality is directing your life, you will more fully appreciate the truth that right purposeful thoughts bring blessings to you; while the habit of indulging in poisonous thoughts of greed, jealousy, criticism, meanness, hatred and despair, will bring misery and dissatisfaction into your life.

*   *   *

So guard the character of your thinking and train your will in goodness and stability if you desire to achieve harmony and success.

*   *   *

"The Lord knoweth the thoughts of men." (Psalm xciii. 11.)

PUT OFF THE OLD MAN

SELF-KNOWLEDGE, self-mastery and self-education are necessary if you wish to change the character of your thinking.

The maxim "Know Thyself" which was inscribed in the Temple of Apollo, at Delphi, is a fundamental principle in character-building; and, as has been said, you can acquire Self-Knowledge, in varying degrees—through reflection upon Jesus' counsels and *an honest check-up upon yourself.*

＊　　　＊　　　＊

Self-mastery can only be attained by struggling until your will is very strong, strong enough to enable you to retain the thoughts that will help you to reach your goal.

＊　　　＊　　　＊

For self-education, you should know something about the workings of the mind.

The developed human mind is inquisitive, —continually seeking answers to its questionings. Consciously or subconsciously it is forever active, never at rest. It is inclined to be vain, egotistical, uncontrolled and aggressive.

It must be made calm, ennobled, and strengthened by self-discipline, if you want to make your life worthy, interesting and fruitful. "Let that Mind be in you, which was also in Christ Jesus." (Phil. ii. 5.)

*　　*　　*

St. Augustine tells us: "God hath created man's mind, rational and intellectual, whereby he may take in His light."

So through strength of character you must put aside your undisciplined self,— *"Stripping (yourself) of the old man with his deeds and putting on the new, him who is renewed unto knowledge according to the image of Him that created him."* (Col. iii. 9, 10.)

Put off "the old man" not by hurried impatient effort, but by gently and faithfully turning aside destructive thoughts in order to apply Jesus' teachings and thus cooperate with your greatest good.

To develop a strong personality, to cast off your old misguided self, to remove faults of character and replace them with virtues, will not be too strenuous a task when self-discipline is aided by prayer,—*prayer made perfect,—by Humility—Faith—Hope—and Love.*

*   *   *

As you become more enlightened and spiritually awakened, life, for you, will become a most interesting adventure because you will be—"doers of the Word and not hearers only." (James i. 22.)

THOUGHT PRECEDES ACCOMPLISHMENT

IN working toward your desired goal, you can be helped by studying the lives of people who have attained a worthy success.

You will then learn, I am sure, that they had in common a great interest in their objectives, a proper evaluation of themselves, the quality of alertness, a spirit of quietness and tenacity of purpose.

They all used the power of concentration, and they possessed a great Faith.

*　　　*　　　*

Remember, all intellectual and moral improvement, — every scientific, literary and artistic advancement,—in fact, every human accomplishment, before it was manifested, was first a thought in some person's mind.

*　　　*　　　*

A valuable achievement is always costly and the higher the achievement the greater the price. For thought, patient work, a strong will and an active Faith always precede accomplishment.

*   *   *

Achievement usually comes step by step. *So let each day's living be a right step toward your purpose in life.*

*   *   *

It has been said with truth "Genius is the ability to take infinite pains."

YOUR INDIVIDUAL PLACE

"LIFE expresses itself in activity." And "it is not only in the field of knowledge that man would resemble God, he would also bear a resemblance to Him in the field of action." *

"God is Pure Act." ** And because man is made to the image and likeness of God, man desires a life of activity and longs for an opportunity through which he can find the fullest expression for his faculties.

Many people seem to be ignorant of the fact that, at Creation, God had a plan for every individual and that He gave to each one of us the special mental, emotional and physical capacities needed to carry out His plan.

St. Augustine tells us: "Not only heaven and earth, not only man and angel, even the bowels of the lowest animal, even the wing of the bird, the flower of the plant, the leaf of the tree, hath God endowed with every *fitting detail* of their nature."

---

* *Why the Cross,* by Edward Leen, C.S.Sp.
** St. Thomas.

And in the words of St. Thomas, *"God has immediate provision over everything because He has in His Intellect the plans of everything, even the smallest. . . . "*

*   *   *

The knowledge that God has provided for each one a vocation which will satisfy the individual's inner yearning should bring into every life a strong spirit of Hope, Courage and Security.

At present, your life may be perplexed and confused because you have failed to find the place that God has prepared for you.

However, it will be less difficult for you to determine your desired activity if you follow the instruction given by St. Augustine, that is: "Recognize in thyself something within. Descend into thyself. Go to thy secret chamber, thy mind," that you may know your capabilities; your weaknesses; whether or not you procrastinate and drift instead of having a well-organized plan for carrying out your vocation; whether or not you are aware of and honestly admit your deep-rooted convictions and their effect both upon yourself and your dealings with others.

*   *   *

Success or failure may depend upon your attitude toward life and people. Is it your belief that life owes you something without any contribution from you? Would you, if necessary, hurt another to gain you own advantage? Does life mean only pleasure? Or is it essential to your happiness to use your innate ability? Do you contribute your "bit" in service toward your fellow man?

It is also important for you to recognize the connection between the state of your mentality and your outer condition. Do you see and acknowledge your own responsibility and shortcomings? To what extent do *your* thoughts, words and actions make your present situation?

If your life contains a difficulty there is through it, a lesson to be learned and mastered before you can progress. So with wisdom and tolerance make the effort to see your present happenings in their true light.

As you *"recognize in thyself something within,"* The Inner Voice, The Inspiration of God, will reveal to you your hidden powers and show you how to use them. *Then according to your patience, your power of concentration, your tenacity of purpose and your Faith, it will be done unto you.*

For Divine Wisdom, with your cooperation, will guide you to the rich opportunities that He has prepared for you and which are awaiting your acceptance.

*   *   *

When you finally win your individual place, you will have found happiness, because the avenue opened up to you will be in harmony with your temperament and will furnish a most satisfying expression for your innate ability,—your special gift from God.

Your willingness to graciously accept God's plan will bring you His Blessing, and with it the ability to fill your place, however lowly it may seem, with distinction and joy, *because you will know that you are functioning as an instrument of God.*

"CIVILIZATION IS IN THE PRINCIPLES THAT GUIDE THE MIND"

THIS wonderful world so full of beauty and the opportunity for joy is in chaos. And as surely as man's wrong thinking caused it man's right thinking can change it.

"Hear thou My son and be wise and guide thy mind in the way." (Prov. xxiii. 19.)

For it is through the power of thought that human wills are invited to move.

We must face the very interesting fact that the intrinsic character of the world's future is depending upon what the masses will think today,—tomorrow,—and the days that follow.

Therefore it is not enough for the individual to guide his own mind "in the way" but it is his Christian duty to endeavor to teach others to have their minds turned Godward,— the true way of living,—and thus help to bring about a Christian world.

"God is the cause of goodness in others; and so the creature becomes like God by moving others to be good." *

When all humanity follows the teachings of Jesus, there will be superior civilization and great happiness in the world.

"But when will ye learn that civilization is not primarily of the body but of the soul,—that civilization is in the principles that guide the mind." **

St. Augustine tells us, "In the mind was man made to the image of God." So every effort must be made to bring the thoughts and attitudes of all mankind in tune with God's Mind, so that the human race may grow more into His Likeness and follow His Way.

Then little by little all minds would be cleansed from false thinking, enlightened and filled to overflowing with God's Wisdom and Goodness.

*   *   *

When all men have a spirit of generosity and cooperation the way will be prepared for

---

* St. Thomas.
** Father Martin J. O'Malley, "The Catholic Hour."

fruitful opportunities and contentment to come into every life.

*   *   *

"God enlightens by changing the intellect and will; He cleanses by removing defects of intellect and will." *

*   *   *

"Submit thyself, then, to Him and be at peace; and thereby thou shalt have the best fruits." (Job xxii. 21.)

------

* St. Thomas.

GOD IN HIS RIGHTFUL PLACE

BECAUSE of business, family cares, or the numerous calls of life, it may not be possible for you to give a major part of your time to spiritual devotions, or to helping others in their efforts to understand and live a true Christian life.

The first commandment states: *"Thou shalt not have strange gods before Me."*

So if you cannot find time from business, pleasure, reading, movies, bridge, or golf to give at least a half hour each day to thank God for His Blessings and to consult Him about your problems, then, indeed, have you placed "strange gods" before Him.

But when through persistent effort you do not allow love of self or of any person, place or thing, however worthy, to keep you from obeying God's Commandment your life will be in order,—harmonious, purposeful and joyous, because God will hold first place.

In the New Law, you may learn Jesus'
Great Commandment of Love: *"Thou shalt
love the Lord thy God, . . . with thy whole
mind, and with thy whole strength."*
(Mark xii. 30.)

*　　*　　*

The second commandment of Love is like
unto the first: *"Thou shalt love thy neighbor
as thyself."*

*　　*　　*

The following are also Commandments
of Love: "Love one another as I have loved
you"; "If ye have aught against any man,
forgive"; "Renounce the hidden things of
dishonesty"; "The Lord hateth a lying
tongue."

*　　*　　*

"If you know these things, you shall be
blessed if you do them."　(John xiii. 17.)

GOD'S NATURE

ALL life, beauty, wisdom, knowledge, goodness and love are forever proceeding from the Mind and Will of God.

For God is the Source of Life; the Source of Beauty; the Source of Truth; the Source of Love; the Source of Goodness.

And God's plan for you is that you should receive in abundance all these gifts which proceed from Him.

So do not allow your thoughts or actions to prevent God's Goodness from benefiting you. But open your mind to The Mind of God that you may receive from The Source the help you need.

*   *   *

The essence of what is called "The Supernatural Life" * consists in knowing the Nature of God and His Laws; also in striving to know His Plan and endeavoring to do His Holy Will.

---

* The Supernatural phase of existence will be considered in Part II.

It is because man so foolishly persists in following his own way of selfishness, greed and hatred that the human race progresses so slowly toward the fulfillment of God's Plan; therefore, because of ignorance and self-centeredness, humanity, in general, is not ready to receive of God's Goodness and Love.

*   *   *

The Catechism will tell you: "God made you to know Him, to love Him, and to serve Him in this life, in order that you may be happy with Him forever in the next."

To Know God—fills one with a zest for living. For as you grow in appreciation of the true Nature of God, realizing, that He has a care for you individually and sends what in His Love He knows is best for your advancement, you will desire to love Him.

To Love God—will bring you the joy of peace, the serenity of true humility and a keen desire to serve Him at all times.

"Let us not love in word nor in tongue, but in deed, and in truth." (1 John iii. 18).

To Serve God—through love, in either a small or magnificent way, makes life complete.

*   *   *

If your good deeds to your fellow men have not received recognition, realize that while the individual you helped may not have shown appreciation, nevertheless every good deed is rewarded.

"Life is a boomerang." What you send out in thought, word or deed will, in time, return to you.

In any of life's interests if you give little, you will receive little; if you give much, much will return to you. *"He who soweth sparingly, shall also reap sparingly: and he who soweth in blessings, shall also reap blessings."* (2 Cor. ix. 6.)

*   *   *

The more time and study you give to your Religion, the more joy you will receive from its truth and beauty.

You will realize, too, that it is the spiritually developed who possess most attractive traits of character,—whose achievements are best for humanity,—whom the world most respects and honors,—and who enjoy a purposeful life of Beauty, Truth and Achievement.

TRUE HUMILITY BRINGS WISDOM

HUMILITY is the foundation for all spiritual growth. It signifies openness of mind and a willingness to learn.

Humility has nothing to do with being rich or poor—learned or uninformed.

There is nothing servile about humility; rather it gives one dignity.

True humility comes from not allowing self to receive undue attention.

As you put God first in your life and grow in an understanding of His Goodness, His Purity, and His Mercy you will naturally become more humble.

If you are truly humble, you will value your gifts as coming from God's Hand; you will give thanks and praise to God for them; and desiring to be more like God, you, too, will be generous with your gifts—time—money—and kindness.

By His Life, Jesus taught us that true

humility always promotes a longing to do God's Will.

Realizing so perfectly and lovingly that He was the Son of God, Jesus fulfilled the prophecy: *"It is written of Me that I should do Thy Will, O God."* (Heb. x. 7.)

When we realize that we are God's children, like Jesus, we, too, will long to do the Will of the Father, knowing that by so doing we will grow nearer to His Likeness and achieve our true destiny.

*   *   *

"The Magnificat" sung by the Mother of Jesus explains true humility.

My soul doth magnify the Lord, and my spirit hath rejoiced in God my Saviour because He hath regarded the humility of His Handmaid; for behold from henceforth, all generations shall call me blessed. Because He That Is Mighty, hath done great things to me; and Holy Is His Name. . . . He hath put down the mighty from their seat, and hath exalted the humble." (Luke i. 46-52).

THINKING WITH GOD

From our enemies:

> from our unseen foes the devils who hate
> us . . .
>
> from wicked men who plot our ruin . . .
>
> from our downward-trending nature . . .
>
> from our bad habits we have contracted . . .

Deliver us:

> of ourselves we are weak . . .
>
> of ourselves we are an easy prey to our
> enemies within and without . . .
>
> of ourselves we readily tire of good . . .
>
> and so we need God's help and grace.

O God—

> in no other can we have final confidence . . .
>
> on no other can we lean unreservedly . . .
>
> for no other has complete power to help . . .
>
> from no other can we expect all-embracing
> mercy . . . *

---

* By the Rev. Francis P. LeBuffe, S.J., in *The Queen's Work*.
(Page 37)

RENUNCIATION

If thou couldst empty all thyself of self

Like to a shell dishabited

Then might He find thee on the ocean shelf

And say: "This is not dead"

And fill thee with Himself instead.

But thou art all replete with only thou

And hast such shrewd activity

That when He comes He says:

"This is enow unto itself

'Twere better let it be

It is so small and full there is no room for
Me." *

---

* Author unknown.

SOUL ACTIVITY

"THE Name, He who is, is most properly applied to God, for it signifies existence itself." *

When we speak of "being" we mean something having existence.

"Every being exists according to some form," *—minerals, vegetables, animals, human beings, angels.

"God is the most noble of beings." * *"He is the Fount and principle of all being."* *

*   *   *

Human beings have a bodily life, a spiritual life,—that of the intellect and will,—and the possibility of a Supernatural Life.**

The Catechism tells us that human beings are composed of body and soul. . . .

*   *   *

Your bodily life should receive proper

---

* St. Thomas.
** The term "spiritual life" as used in this pamphlet does not refer to the Supernatural Life, but only to the natural activity of the mind and will.

attention. In fact, it should be made as healthy as possible.

But the development of your spiritual faculties,—your intellect and your will,—should receive even more attention because they are of a higher order and determine your interests and progress in life.

* * *

Your soul functions through its rational faculties,—intellect and will; and through your sense life,—seeing, hearing, imaginings, memories, feelings, passions (love, hate, hope, fear, joy, sadness, indignation, etc.).

* * *

The soul of each human being is the center of his inner life, which includes his spiritual, emotional and Supernatural activities.

* * *

So with the Psalmist you should sing: *"Bless the Lord, O my soul, and never forget all He hath done for thee."* (cii. 2.)

YOUR WILL

YOUR will is the seat of desire. It is an ever-present power which can be used to bring about your happiness or your misery.

Because your will has the power to choose and to act, it can accept or reject what is presented to it by the intellect.

"The will moves the intellect to its operation." * Therefore it is through your will that you control your life.

To quote from St. Augustine: "It is the will by which we sin or live well."

* * *

Every human being desires satisfaction through the attainment of his heart's desire— the thing which seems most necessary for his happiness.

* * *

In the pursuit of happiness your will might choose recreation, wealth or power because, at the time, they seemed to you most desirable.

The possession of wealth or power, if used

---

* St. Thomas.

properly, need contain no evil. They are indeed worthy when acquired honestly, held in their proper places, and used for good purposes.

However, the attaining of these desires should never be regarded as the ultimate achievement.

*   *   *

The "Pride of Power" and the "Love of Money" are the real dangers to be avoided.

TOOLS FOR ACHIEVING

YOUR intellect and your will are the most important powers of your soul,— your best tools, in achieving your desired goal. So, they should be both developed and strengthened by constant exercise.

However, as these vital powers belong to human nature, they have an inherent tendency to make self the greatest interest. This causes restlessness, instability and unbalanced judgments.

So no matter how brilliant the intellect or how strong the will, for true permanent success, human effort needs the Divine Help.

As St. Thomas points out: *"The rational creature governs itself by its intellect and will, both of which require to be governed and perfected by the Divine Intellect and Will."*

The education of your intellect and will is most necessary for intelligent productive living.

But furthermore, your will and your intellect, being the powers of your soul, are purely spiritual and will never die. They will function forever. That is, for all eternity your soul will live and you will use the same intellect and will you now have.

And this is what is meant by the immortality of the soul.

*　　*　　*

Therefore, education to fulfill its highest purpose should give an understanding and appreciation of the Supernatural Life, because unless you live according to Supernatural Laws your life upon earth will not be satisfactory and you cannot have a joyous eternity.

"Now this is eternal life: that they may know Thee, the only true God, and Jesus Christ, whom Thou hast sent." (John xvii. 3.)

And with this knowledge of God, there should be a staunch unwavering conviction that Jesus keeps His promises.

GOD IS SUPREME INTELLECT AND SUPREME WILL

ST. THOMAS tells us: *"God's Life is in His Intellect and in His Will."*

And because you are made to the image and likeness of God your spiritual growth depends upon the combined action of your intellect and your will; your Supernatural growth upon this same activity guided by the Light of Faith.

Your intellect gives you the power to think and it is the nature of the intellect to be forever seeking knowledge with the hope of finding the ultimate truth.

Your will gives you the power to discriminate, to love, to control. And it is the nature of the will to be restless—ever seeking for the fulfillment of its desires.

God never forces your will for He wants you a free agent.

God's great gift of free will raises you to a high dignity, but brings grave responsibility because it makes you accountable for your actions.

* * *

So consider carefully your decisions and your sustained will-activity in accomplishing these decisions, since it is possible for you to overcome most of your difficulties and to win high achievement through the carrying out of right choices.

* * *

In the words of St. Augustine: "If they desire power they shall be masters of their wills even as God is Master of His Will."

"HEAR THE VOICE OF THE LORD THY GOD"

*   *   *

"I HAVE SET BEFORE THEE THIS DAY LIFE AND GOOD AND ON THE OTHER HAND DEATH AND EVIL."

*   *   *

"CHOOSE LIFE THAT BOTH THOU AND THY SEED MAY LIVE. DO MANFULLY BE OF GOOD HEART FEAR NOT NOR BE YE DISMAYED . . . FOR THE LORD THY GOD HE, HIMSELF IS THY LEADER AND WILL NOT LEAVE THEE NOR FORSAKE THEE!"

(Deuteronomy xxx. 8, 15, 19; xxxi. 6.)

PART II

"EYE HATH NOT SEEN
NOR EAR HEARD
NEITHER HATH IT ENTERED
INTO THE HEART OF MAN,
WHAT THINGS
GOD HATH PREPARED
FOR THEM THAT LOVE HIM"

(1 Corinthians ii. 9.)

THE GIFT OF BAPTISM

IT will help you greatly to know about an even higher and more sacred truth than that of your human existence,—The Gift of Baptism,—the deep significance of which is not always grasped.

For through the power of the Love, Obedience and Suffering offered by Jesus, our Divine Brother, you were raised, at Baptism, from a natural to a Divine Plane.

You were made "a partaker of the Divine Nature." (2 Peter i. 4.)

Then in very truth you were "Born again not of corruptible seed but incorruptible." (1 Peter i 23.)

And this Divine Seed implanted in the depths of your soul gave to your human faculties a Divine Impetus enabling you to participate in the Supernatural Divine Life.

Therefore you were made more truly to God's Own Image and Likeness.

And **through the growth of this hidden**

incorruptible Seed, greater and greater blessings will come to you.

"As the earth is powerless to rise till the seed, bringing a new and mysterious force into it, seizes upon those elements in it which yield themselves to its influence and transforms and raises them, so it is with this Divine Seed cast into the soil of human nature. It enters as a new force into our nature." *

*   *   *

The glory of your human nature is your intellect and your will given you by God at the moment of your creation.

But through the Divine Seed,—the gift of Sanctifying Grace,—your intellect and will receive the power to perform Godlike acts and "The eternal glorification of the body is . . . here below prepared and established." **

"This increase of the intellectual powers is called the illumination of the intellect" by St. Thomas.

---

* *Self-Knowledge and Self-Discipline*, Rev. B. W. Marturin.
** Nicholas Gihr.

"THE SUPERNATURAL LIFE"

YOUR Supernatural Divine Life which was given you at Baptism, should be your greatest interest; *because its development is the most important phase of your existence.*

"It is evidently not sufficient that we exist. We have work to do, things to get done, steps to take, for in the Supernatural as well as in the natural order it is equally true that we carve our own destiny with the tools of our human actions." *

To quote from St. Augustine: "The knowledge of the natural man is through reason: of the man placed by Sanctifying Grace in the Supernatural Order it is Faith."

Many devout, simple souls, through their deep Faith and Love of God, know intuitively that a complete cooperation with His Will brings the blessing of a greater participation in the Supernatural Life. But others, less favored, need to study the laws of the Super-

---

* *A Companion to the Summa,* Rev. Walter Farrell, O.P.

natural Life, before they can understand that of they wish to enjoy Supernatural growth and privileges it is necessary to follow God's Will.

*   *   *

The great spiritual writers St. Augustine, St. Thomas, St. John of the Cross, St. Theresa of Avila, St. Therese of Lisieux and many others are an inexhaustible source of information and inspiration.

Their books explaining the higher life are so surprisingly fascinating that they give an impetus to seek further enlightenment. And as Supernatural knowledge increases, there is an enthusiastic desire to devote more time and energy to the development of the Divine Seed implanted at Baptism.

"It is the seed that reveals to the earth its latent powers, wakens them and uses them. So does Grace reveal man to himself. Coming, into his nature it shows him what he can be, new uses to which his powers can be put, new combinations, new developments." *

-----

* *Self-Knowledge and Self-Discipline,* Rev. B. W. Maturin.

(Page 54)

St. Thomas tells us "God is within us in three ways: By His power, by His presence, and by His essence." The Spirit of God Who, in the natural order, gave us the power to walk, to talk, to think, will (when we believe and respond to grace) quicken our mind and strengthen our will in order that we can recognize and use His power, within us, for our highest development. Jesus said: *"If Thou canst believe* all things are possible to him that believeth." (Mark ix. 22.)

St. Augustine tells us that *"God satisfies the seeker in the measure of his capacity and He makes the finder to have greater capacity so that he may again seek to be filled when his ability to receive has grown."*

* * *

Live each day a little better than the day before in honesty, truth, Faith, and Love, that your "ability to receive" may grow.

* * *

LET US PRAY
Soul of my soul send forth Thy Spirit, "enliven what is dead, inundate my being with a flood-tide of Thy Grace."

LIFE—TRUTH—LOVE

THE gift of prayer will help you greatly to draw from God a deeper participation in the Supernatural Life. But the most substantial and glorious way that the Divine Seed can be nourished in your soul and your capacity for receiving God's Gift increased is by partaking of The Holy Eucharist with true humility and love.

Jesus said, *"The Bread that I will give, is My Flesh, for the Life of the world,"* (John vi. 53) referring, of course, not to the natural, but to the Supernatural Life.

He also said, *"He that eateth My Flesh, and drinketh My Blood hath everlasting life; and I will raise him up on the last day."* (John vi. 52.)

*　　*　　*

One of the underlying principles of Christianity is "Brotherly Love," in recognition of the truth that every faithful follower of Jesus is a God-bearer and should manifest Truth and Love.

St. Thomas, the profound exponent of Jesus' teachings, tell us: "The Whole Trinity Dwells in the Mind by Sanctifying Grace."

The Father,—Life; The Indwelling Christ,—Truth; The Holy Spirit,—Love.

"SEEK YE THE LORD AND LIVE"

(Amos v. 4, 6.)

AS your intellect becomes more fully illumined through the Light of God's Grace, you will, with greater Faith, seek to know God and His Laws.

And as your will becomes more deeply influenced through your participation in the Divine Nature, you will desire to make the right choices. You will also long to grow in the love of God.

Then as your will becomes stronger through your right choices and is expanding in the love of God because of your conscious cooperation with His inspirations, you will continuously reach out and yearn for a deeper Union with God,—the Source of Divine Wisdom—Energy—and Love.

With the Psalmist, you may then truly exclaim: *"As the hart panteth after the fountains of waters, so my soul panteth after Thee O God."* (Psalm xli. 2.)

Many people who have achieved wealth, honor and distinction are still dissatisfied. But they continue to seek for contentment or happiness through these means—not realizing that the attainment they are really striving for is to enjoy Union with God—which is the All-Satisfying ultimate achievement.

"For however great the goods of these worlds of nature, they are puny substitutes to an intellect thirsting for supreme truth, to an appetite that only the universal good will ever satisfy." *

* * *

Because St. Augustine understood so well this restlessness of the human will he wrote: *"Thou hast created me for Thyself, O God, and my heart will know no peace, until it rests in Thee."*

---

* *A Companion to the Summa,* by Walter Farrell, O.P.

THE TEMPLE OF THE LIVING GOD

"KNOW you not, that you are the temple of God, and that The Spirit of God dwelleth in you?" (1 Cor. iii. 16.)

For when you are participating in the Supernatural Life, the Holy Spirit is present in the depths of your being with His great Power-giving Gifts, Wisdom, Understanding, Counsel, Knowledge, Fortitude, Piety and Holy Fear.

Then, as the Beloved Apostle, St. John, said: *"Greater is He that is in you than he that is in the world."* (1 John iv. 4.)

The Holy Spirit dwelling within you, is awaiting the conscious cooperation of your illumined and transformed mind that He may bring you into an interior union with His Own Radiant Presence, and He is awaiting the gradual turning of your strengthened will away from self to the full acceptance of His Holy Will, *that your will and His Will may meet and become one.*

(Page 60)

While, with your whole being you are consciously reaching out for *Contact with The Holy Spirit* you will more deeply realize that the secret of happy living is to manifest the Fruits of the Spirit ("Charity, Joy, Peace, Patience, Kindness, Goodness, Faithfulness, Gentleness, Self-Control" *) — *Christlike qualities which when exemplified,* will bring God's Blessing.

And with His Blessing all good things will follow.

Only a character of such integrity can live a life of purpose and achievement, well pleasing to God.

*   *   *

"Be ye filled with The Holy Spirit."
(Eph. v. 18.)

*   *   *

St. Anthony who manifested the Fruits of the Spirit and successfully reached the Heart of God prayed for *the Greatest Gift—The Holy Presence*—in the following words:

---

* Gal. v. 23.

ST. ANTHONY'S PRAYER

"O Light of the world, Infinite God, Father of Eternity, Giver of Wisdom and Knowledge! . . . Stretch forth Thy Hand

And put Thy Spirit, O Lord in my heart, that I may understand and retain what I learn and meditate on it in my heart.

Do Thou lovingly, holily, mercifully, clemently, and gently inspire me with Thy Grace.

Do Thou teach, guide and strengthen the thoughts of my mind. . . .

May the counsel of The Most High Help Me, Through Thy Infinite Wisdom and Mercy. Amen."

CONTACT WITH THE HOLY SPIRIT

WHEN through the exercise of deeper Faith, Hope and Love, you attain an ever closer Contact with The Holy Spirit, This Divine One dwelling within you will pour into your mind in greater abundance The Light of His Own Radiance and into your will His Love and Power.

Thus your intellect will be given a new impetus, a new power, a supreme available help.

And "for the mind to attain to God, in some degree, is great beatitude." *

Your will's restlessness will then cease, and you will know a serenity and peace that is satisfying.

"In this Contact with God and intimacy with Him is found that happiness for which man was created and for which he craves." **

---

* St. Thomas.

** *Why the Cross*, Edward Leen, C.S.Sp.

With the consciousness of this Holy Presence and His Powerful Help, you will bravely meet your problems without fear or confusion, and overcome them with confidence and ability.

"God hath girded me with strength and made my way perfect." (2 Kings xxii. 33.)

*   *   *

As The Holy Spirit, The Reservoir of Love and All-Good, fills a human will with His peace and power, that person experiences in the depths of his being (soul) a constant urge to keep sacred this joyous power-giving contact, untouched by the inharmonies and pressure of life.

IT IS GOD WHO WORKETH IN YOU

THROUGH the constant loving aware-
ness of the Holy and All-Powerful
Presence within you and the offering of yourself to His Guidance.

You will experience an earthly Heaven.

*　　*　　*

You will rejoice in knowing that
*"It is God who worketh in you both the
will and the performance to fulfil His good
pleasure."* (Phil. ii.13.)

And you will enjoy an ever deeper realization of the richness in meaning contained
in the following truths:

"It hath pleased Your Father to give You
a Kingdom." (Luke xii. 32.) And "The Kingdom of God is within You." (Luke xvii. 21.)

Day by day—hour by hour—at every critical moment, you will turn with complete Faith to the Holy Spirit within you, knowing that you can obtain in full measure:

> The *Wisdom* you need for guidance;
>
> The *Power* you need for achievement;
>
> The *Answer* to your life's problems;
>
> The *Peace* of mind you need for serenity;

*   *   *

"Seek ye therefore first the Kingdom of God and His Justice and all these things shall be added unto you." (Matt vi. 33.)

LOVE, ACHIEVEMENT, SERVICE

WITH praise and thanksgiving, you will pray to The Holy Spirit, asking that you may always keep uppermost in your consciousness His nearness and availability.

You will be ever alert in order to recognize the Inspirations coming from your Divine Counsellor.

You will pray as Cardinal Mercier prayed:

"O Holy Spirit, beloved of my soul,
I adore Thee.

Enlighten me, guide me, strengthen me,
console me.

Tell me what Thou wouldst have me to do."

Through your trueness to The Holy Spirit, together with good will toward all, the highest and best avenue for your achievement and service will be opened to you.

Thus you will be among the confident happy people on this earth, who know with certainty that God's Plan for them, *is a complete and joyous life of* Love, Achievement, Service, and Success by The Spiritual Way.

TO THE HOLY SPIRIT

GREAT Holy One, dwelling within my soul: help me to speak with Thee, casting out all natural and human reflections.

Let my soul feel Thy Divine Touch and be drawn into oneness with Thee.

Thou hast said: "He that soweth in his flesh, of the flesh also shall reap corruption. *But he that soweth in the Spirit of the Spirit shall reap life everlasting.*" (Gal. vi. 8, 9.)

"O Lord My God, My Holy One!" Thou dost possess a very fullness of Divine Life. And I pray Thee, fill my entire being with this Life of Thine. Take full possession of me.

In Thy Purity, Thy Power, Thy Wisdom, and Thy Love operate in me and through me to glorify Thyself—doing good as Thou wilt.

Then, in very truth, I shall have sown "in the Spirit,"—the path of my life here upon earth shall be strewn with good,—and I "shall reap life everlasting."

PART III

"IF YOU CONTINUE IN MY WORD,
YOU SHALL BE MY DISCIPLES IN-
DEED. AND YOU SHALL KNOW THE
TRUTH, AND THE TRUTH SHALL
MAKE YOU FREE."

(John viii. 31, 32.)

"AWAKE, THOU THAT SLEEPEST"

(Eph. v. 14.)

THE Indians had the first opportunity to make the gold mines of America their own. But they did not know of their existence, consequently, they could not grasp this opportunity.

But the white man had learned of the existence of these mines, so he made them yield him every material luxury.

*   *   *

At the present time, many people are missing a much greater treasure than rich material gold-fields. For they are missing the resources of their inner world. *They are not digging into the depths of truth.* They are living on the surface!

But through Jesus' Teachings, you know of the existence of Your Greatest Gift—The Holy Spirit within you.

So be wise, dig deep, seek The All-Good, and thus make your life useful, interesting and complete.

"GRIEVE NOT THE HOLY SPIRIT OF GOD"

(Eph. iv. 30.)

AFTER Baptism, by wrong thinking,— wrong action,—or by ignoring His Sacred Presence (venial sin),—the action of The Holy Spirit abiding within you may be lessened.

Thus your intellect and will can lose much of their inspiration and energy.

By sinning gravely (mortal sin), you cannot possess the Divine Light.

We are told *"The lamp of the wicked shall be put out."* (Prov. xiii. 9.)

Should the action of The Holy Spirit dwelling within you, cease entirely, conditions in your inner world would become dark and dreary.

For the Light of Grace would not be present in your soul!

Then you would no longer possess the steady Divine contact,—the expensive gift Jesus gave His Life to buy for you.

Consequently, sin—lack and misery— would be your experience.

*   *   *

"For which cause I admonish thee, that thou stir up the Grace of God which is in thee." (2 Tim. i. 6.)

THE CONDITION OF YOUR INNER WORLD

THE condition of your inner world always affects your outer world, because the thoughts of your mind and the acts of your will contribute greatly toward making your health, disposition, environment and achievement what it is.

*　　*　　*

It is natural in life to meet with obstacles and problems. They are needed for spiritual growth.

Yet to overcome your difficulties may seem to you like a big task, because of the necessity of controlling the action of your intellect and will both of which may be weakened by unresisted temptation — procrastination—indolence—and unstable habits.

*　　*　　*

However, thousands of people are succeeding in controlling their thoughts and actions. And with intelligence and strength of will you can do likewise.

The fruit resulting from this accomplishment is well worth the effort.

For we are told: *"He that shall overcome. . . . I will not blot out his name out of the Book of Life and I will confess his name before My Father."* (Apoc. iii. 5.)

So have confidence. You can succeed.

*   *   *

Use right thinking, self-discipline, obedience to the Divine Commandments, and prayer to lead you to The Source of Light and Strength.

PRAYER, THE INSPIRATION OF HIGH ACHIEVEMENT

THE power of true prayer is tremendous. It is the dynamo of the spiritual world. Through it, your mind is brought into contact with the Mind of God whereby you may give Him praise, love and thanksgiving. And you may also ask Him for your every need.

Dr. Alexis Carrel the eminent scientist wrote: "It is by prayer that man reaches God and that God enters into him. Prayer appears to be indispensable to our highest development. We should not look upon prayer as an act in which only the weak-minded, the beggars or cowards indulge. In fact it is no more shameful to pray than to drink or to breathe. Man needs God as he needs water and oxygen. Joined to intuition, to the moral sense, to the sense of the beautiful and to the light of intelligence, *the sense of the holy gives to the personality its full flowering.**

---

* Prayer by Dr. Alexis Carrel, Morehouse-Gotham Co., Publishers.

Jesus, who understood best the power of prayer, repeatedly and emphatically counselled, "Pray without ceasing." (1 Thess. v. 17.) Also "Whatsoever you shall ask in prayer, Believing, you shall receive." (Matt. xxi. 22.) So when you ask for help and guidance always pray with confidence.

Just saying words is not prayer.

Shakespeare expressed the idea in his play, *Hamlet*: * "My words fly up, my thoughts remain below; words without thought never to heaven go."

Realizing that you are not alone but in communion with the Holy Spirit, consciously examine your thoughts, your desires, your motives, and determine whether they are helpful to yourself and to others, and pleasing to the Lord.

"Draw nigh to God, and He will draw nigh to you." (James iv. 8.)

---

* Act III, Scene III.

If your thoughts are confused or troublesome, let The Holy Spirit speak for you because, "The Spirit also helpeth our infirmity. . . . We know not what we should pray for as we ought; *but the Spirit Himself, asketh for us with unspeakable groanings.*" (Romans viii. 26.)

And the Comforter "He will teach you all things, and bring all things to your mind. . . . "   (John xiv. 26.)

*   *   *

So keep your mind quiet that The Holy Spirit may pray through you and open your mind to The Mind of The Father, thus making your prayer perfect.

MEDITATION

THERE are different types of prayer. And it is The Holy Spirit who will enlighten and guide you through Vocal, Meditative, and Contemplative Prayer, to that of Highest Union with God.

To open the way for peace of mind and a well-ordered life, faults of character must be removed and replaced by virtues. And it is through the type of prayer called Meditation or Mental Prayer that you can most truly discover the faults in your character, learn to know your real self, and find your true place in life according to God's Plan.

*   *   *

You may think that Meditation is something mysterious or complicated. But in reality, it is only thinking for a period of time about one truth or thing from different angles.

For instance, when without interruption, you consider God's Goodness—His Love—His Power—His Availability—His Forgiveness—

and the hopes that you have of winning and enjoying His Blessing, you are then Meditating on God, which would, of course, preclude thoughts of business, pleasure or other subjects.

Concentration, like this, requires some degree of self control and those who have not the habit of self-mastery, will indeed, find some difficulty. *For when one thought is being considered, thoughts about other things must be turned aside.*

If through reflection, you find that you are given to being irritable or easily hurt, then meditate for ten minutes each day upon the Life of Jesus. Recall His Patience, His Humility, His Calmness, His Kindness and the way in which He bore abuse and lack of recognition.

Then, throughout the day, should your feelings be hurt or should you be tempted to show irritability, turn your thoughts away from self, saying: "This must not disturb me, because I am trying to grow more perfectly into the Likeness of Jesus."

If you handle any fault of character in this same way, the annoying condition will undoubtedly disappear.

Perhaps the fear that such results would be "too good to be true" might keep you from trying-out this teaching. But test it.

* * *

Select from the following examples the one in which you are most interested. Meditate upon it faithfully for two weeks, and then I think, you will realize the value of watchful thinking and a controlled will.

ARE YOU CONTENTED?

SOME people are discontented because they have never had an outlet for their creative ability; while others are bewildered because they have not found the "Hidden Talent."

God may have given you many outstanding gifts or it may be you have but "the one talent."

If your talent should be hidden, you can find it more easily if you realize that there is an urge in most of us to do something for the common good. So usually your heart's desire points the way to your special ability.

Of course, if the expression of your heart's desire, would lead to wickedness, pure selfishness or merely to entertainment, look deeper "into thyself," *"And thy ears shall hear the word of one admonishing thee behind thy back: this is the way, walk ye in it: and go not aside neither to the right hand, nor to the left."* (Isaias xxx. 21.) For God has given you your talent to lead you to good.

You may think the field of your inspiration too limited or not of sufficient importance. But remember that what may seem unimportant to you might be the very thing you need to learn before God will open your way to a higher accomplishment.

You can find as much beautiful expression, service and satisfaction in doing well the simple things as you would receive from the doing of great things.

The development of a perfect disposition; acts of gracious kindness; or companionship given to an unfortunate person brings contentment into many lives.

Satisfaction comes into other lives through making a beautiful garden; painting a picture; or writing a poem; while still others realize their heart's desire by creating a harmonious home with lovely children or by studying to become more enlightened that they may assist in the spiritual progress of the human race.

"To everyone of us is given Grace, according to the measure of the giving of Christ." (Eph. iv. 7.)

DO YOU PROCRASTINATE?

ONE may have trained his will so that he does not lie or steal and yet not have trained it to do the thing most needed for his advancement.

Procrastination, the habit of putting off a duty until some future time,—is a sure sign of mental laziness and a flabby will.

But, very often, we are not conscious of the particular weakness of the intellect or will which prevents us from being contented or from achieving.

Philosophers and educators tell us that not knowing one's true self is a common failing. Therefore, learn to "know thyself" so that you can make progress.

And when you pray, ask for the grace to perform the acts that will strengthen your intellect and will,—that you may know the good and have the strength to do it.

* * *

"The sluggard willeth and willeth not."
(Prov. xiii. 4.)

"The thoughts of the industrious always bring forth abundance." (Prov. xxi. 5.)

"Desires kill the slothful: for his hands have refused to work at all. He longeth and desireth all the day." (Prov. xxi. 25, 26.)

*   *   *

Read:

Proverbs vi. 9-11	Proverbs xxiv. 30-34	Romans xii. 11
Proverbs x. 4	Eccles. x. 18	Hebrews vi. 11, 12

ARE YOU HONEST?

HONESTY means integrity of mind and will. Consequently, honesty is required for straight thinking and right action. And it is absolutely necessary in the search for God.

If you want to be honest, through and through, there must be no camouflage. You must rid yourself of self-righteousness, pride of opinion, hypocrisy, lying, deceit and fraud.

You may be honest in your dealings with others, but be dishonest in your thought about yourself.

So try to have the courage to be honest with yourself about yourself. For honest thinking brings a great reward.

*　　*　　*

Devise not a lie against thy brother: neither do the like against thy friend. Be not willing to make any manner of lie: for the custom thereof is not good." (Ecclus. vii. 13, 14.)

"A thief is better than a man that is always lying: but both of them shall inherit destruction." (Ecclus. xx. 27.)

"Nor thieves, nor covetous . . . nor extortioners shall possess the Kingdom of God." (1 Cor. vi. 10.)

*   *   *

Read:

Leviticus xix. 11-19, 35, 36

Deuteronomy xxv. 13-16

Proverbs vi. 16-21; xii. 22

Proverbs xi.

Amos viii. 4-6

Zacharias v. 3-11

Romans xiii. 13

1 Cor. vi. 8

Ephesians iv. 24

DO YOU WORRY?

IS it the rent? your work? health? temptation? disgrace? loneliness?

Worry indicates weakness in Faith and causes failure.

It will prevent you from being efficient and leads to ill-health.

Therefore think of God's nearness and make Acts of Faith. Thus, you will fill your mind with the conviction that God will help you.

Exercise your will by affirming your Faith. Stop worrying and let God show you the way.

"If ye have Faith as a grain of mustard seed . . . naught shall be impossible to you." (Matt. xvii. 19.)

*　　*　　*

"Have confidence in the Lord with all thy heart, and lean not upon thy own prudence." (Prov. iii. 5.)

"Who is there among you . . . that hath walked in darkness and hath no light? Let him hope in the name of the Lord, and lean upon his God." (Isaias 1. 10.)

＊　　　＊　　　＊

Read:

Psalm xxxiii. 5
Psalm lv. 5
Matthew xix. 26

Matthew xxi. 21
Mark ix. 16-23
Mark x. 27

Mark xi. 23
Luke xvii. 6
John xiv. 1

ARE YOU JEALOUS?

JEALOUSY is at root selfishness. It shows self-seeking disordered love.

Jealousy is a sin bringing in its trail much misery. For jealous thoughts bring injustice —blindness—and serious soul disease.

Look deep for this sin. Make no excuses. For the devil disguises it!

"Love is strong as death, jealousy as hard as Hell, the lamps thereof are fire and flames." (Canticle of Canticles viii. 6.)

* * *

"Thou shalt not hate thy brother in thy heart. . . . Seek not revenge. . . . Thou shalt love thy friend as thyself. I am the Lord." (Lev. xix. 17, 18.)

"Let no man seek his own but that which is another's as I also in all things please all men, not seeking that which is profitable to myself but to many that they may be saved." (1 Cor. x. 24, 33.)

* * *

Read:

Romans xii. 3-8

1 Corinthians xii. 4-30

2 Corinthians ix. 8, 9

Ephesians iv. 1-13

DO YOU INDULGE IN HARMFUL CRITICISM?

IF you indulge in harmful criticism you are injuring yourself!

You will lose in sincerity, breadth of soul and in friendship.

So begin today to stop harmful, petty or unnecessary criticism.

"Judge not that ye may not be judged." Then your life will be more in accord with justice and truth.

If harmful criticism is your fault pray hard for the Gift of Wisdom. For "Blessed is the man that findeth wisdom." (Prov. iii. 13).

"The wisdom that is from above is . . . full of mercy and good fruits, without judging, without dissimulation." (James iii. 17.)

* * *

"Detract not one another, My brethren. He that detracteth his brother or he that judgeth his brother detracteth the law and judgeth the law. . . .

"There is one Law-giver and Judge that is able to destroy and to deliver."
(James iv. 11, 12.)

"But thou, why judgest thou thy brother? Or thou, why dost thou despise thy brother? For we shall all stand before the Judgment Seat of Christ." (Romans xiv. 10.)

*   *   *

Read:

Matthew vii. 1-5, 12
Mark iv. 24

Luke vi. 31, 37
Romans ii. 1-3

ARE YOU UNFORGIVING?

"TO err is human, to forgive Divine." So to forgive is usually very difficult. Yet Jesus counsels: "Forgive not only up to seven times—but up to seventy times seven."

When you are trying to forgive an injustice do it for the love of God, keeping in mind the truth that "To them that love God all things work together unto good." (Romans viii. 28.) Therefore it is to your eternal advantage to follow Jesus' Counsel.

* * *

"If you will forgive men their offences, your Heavenly Father will forgive you also your offences. But if you will not forgive men neither will your Father forgive you your offences." (Matt. vi. 14, 15.)

"And whensoever ye stand at prayer, forgive if ye have aught against any man, that your Father who is in Heaven may likewise forgive you your transgressions." (Mark xi. 25.)

* * *

Read:

Ecclus. xxviii. 2-6	Matthew vi. 12	Luke vi. 36, 37
Matthew v. 23, 24	Matthew vi. 14, 15	Colossians iii. 12, 13

ARE YOU BITTER?

BITTER thoughts are sickly thoughts. If you want to be healthier in your spiritual outlook, happier and better loved, be cheerful, gracious, more optimistic.

Bitterness shows that you need to grow in understanding so that your thoughts of people and affairs will be correct. "**Judge not according to the appearance, but judge just judgment.**" (John vii. 24.)

* * *

"Pray to God: that perhaps this thought of thy heart may be forgiven thee. For I see thou art in the gall of bitterness, and in the bonds of iniquity." (Acts viii. 22, 23.)

"Let all bitterness . . . and anger . . . and abusive language be removed from you. . . . " (Eph. iv. 31.)

* * *

Read:

Romans iii. 13, 14
Hebrews xii. 14, 15

James iii. 11-15
1 John iv. 7-13

ARE YOU GRASPING?

DO you seek undue attention? Is your desire for power excessive? Do you let material things possess you? Do you crave and exact undue affection?

This soul disease is progressive! A grasping person can never be satisfied. The more he gets the more he wants.

A grasping person is usually self-centered and unhappy.

And Jesus counsels us to beware of all covetousness.

To experience happiness you should recognize all your blessings as gifts. You should give and be thankful for the gift of giving.

* * *

"Take heed, and beware of all covetousness: for a man's life doth not consist in the abundance of things he possesseth."
(Luke xii. 15.)

* * *

Read:

Proverbs x. 6   Matthew vi. 28-34   Luke vi. 38
Proverbs xi. 5, 8   Luke vi. 31   Luke xii. 16-21

ARE YOU AN ALCOHOLIC?

IF you are an alcoholic endeavor to discover the cause. Should your nervous energy be depleted build up your nerves with food and rest. Should you have too much leisure find a hobby which will give you an absorbing interest. In all cases, especially if you are discouraged, pray to obtain spiritual help and a keener sense of the Presence of God.

Do not use alcohol to ease a sorrow or an injustice. Very often a cure is effected by forgetting self, being thoughtful of others, and lending a helping hand. Understand that excessive indulgence in alcoholic drink weakens the will. This makes it difficult to live a useful life—to experience happiness or to bring it to others.

Know that your actions affect both this life and the life hereafter. So practise self-discipline. Strengthen your Faith until you conquer. It can be done.

"Be not drunk with wine, wherein is luxury; but be ye filled with The Holy Spirit." (Eph. v. 18.)

"He that is delighted in passing his time over wine, leaveth a reproach in his Strongholds." (Prov. xii. 1.)

*   *   *

Read:

Proverbs xx. 1	Ecclus. xxxi. 30-42	Romans xiii. 13
Proverbs xxiii. 20, 21	Isaias v. 11	Romans xiv. 21
Proverbs xxiii. 29-32	Luke xxi. 34	Galatians v. 21

ARE YOU SENSUAL?

THE sensual person has not learned the fascination and delights of the Supernatural Life—the life of high purpose and the love of good. Hard work, another interest, high thoughts, unselfishness, will help to divert you from this sin.

Then persistent prayer with frequent Communion will help you to a higher life and the joyous satisfaction of chastity. "The pure of heart . . . see God." (Matt. v. 8.)

* * *

"Dreadful are the ends of a wicked race." (Wis. iii. 19.)

"The Lord beholdeth the ways of man: and considereth all his steps. His own iniquities catch the wicked, and he is fast bound with the ropes of his own sins." (Prov. v. 21, 22.)

"He that soweth in his flesh, from the flesh shall reap destruction." (Gal. vi. 8.)

* * *

Read:

Psalm i. 1-3
Proverbs iii. 1, 2
Proverbs iv. 14, 15

Wisdom iv. 1, 2
Romans vi. 12-23
1 Corinthians vii. 1-19

ARE YOU "SMUG"?

"HEAR, O foolish people, and without understanding, who have eyes and see not: and ears and hear not." (Jer. v. 21.)

If you are smug, you are standing in your own light. You have a closed mind. You are not doing your duty. You are shutting the door of opportunity to yourself and others.

Smug people should realize that conditions change and that very often new ways are an improvement upon the old. So be open-minded and accept the new if it is right.

*　　*　　*

"Be not wise in thy own conceit." (Prov. iii. 7.)

"Woe to you Scribes and Pharisees, hypocrites; . . . blind guides, who strain out a gnat, and swallow a camel." (Matt. xxiii. 23, 24.)

*　　*　　*

Read:

Isaias lviii. 7-11	Luke x. 29-37	Luke xi. 42-51
Matthew xxiii. 23-25	Mark xii. 38-41	Luke xviii. 10-14

(Page 101)

ARE YOU FALSELY SUPERIOR-MINDED?

BE truly superior in as many ways as possible not forgetting the highest culture, that is, to be superior in tolerance, kindness and understanding.

If you are falsely superior-minded you will be blind to your shortcomings and no one will tell you the truth about yourself.

By the fact that you set yourself above others, you are shut off from cooperative work. This isolation brought on by your own mental attitude causes you to become self-pitying and more deeply self-centered.

If you are superior-minded remember: "God resisteth the proud. And giveth grace to the humble." (James iv. 6.)

"I say to each one among you not to think more of himself than he ought to think." (Romans xii. 3.)

*　　*　　*

All good gifts come from God—*"Be not puffed up."* (1 Cor. iv. 6.)

"Nay, what hast thou which thou hast not received? And if thou hast received it, why dost thou glory, as if thou hast not received it?" (1 Cor. iv. 7.)

"Take up My yoke upon you, and learn of Me because I am meek, and humble of heart." (Matt. xi. 29.)

＊　　＊　　＊

Read:

Proverbs iii. 34	Luke xviii. 13, 14	James iv. 6
Matthew vii. 7, 8	1 Corinthians xv. 10	James iv. 15-17
Matthew xv. 25, 27	Ephesians ii. 8-10	1 Peter v. 5

DO NOT FEAR

FREQUENT meditation will show fear to be at the root of most difficulties.

If you want peace of mind, confidence, and achievement, clear your inner world of fear thoughts. For fear often causes what is called an inferiority-complex. It sickens both body and soul.

Some fears lie deeply hidden. But when you discover the cause of your fear and have overcome it through Faith and Prayer, much bitterness, jealousy, grasping, sullenness and unforgiveness will disappear.

But what is known as Holy Fear,— Reverence for God,—is praiseworthy, and it is the beginning of Wisdom.

*   *   *

Jesus, who understood so well that fear lies deep in human hearts, supplied our need of peace. For at the Last Supper with the words "Peace I leave with you, My Peace I give unto you," He bequeathed to us the great Gift— Peace of mind.

Learn to make use of this gift. It was given to you freely and with Divine Love.

*   *   *

"Behold I command thee, take courage, and be strong. Fear not and be not dismayed: because the Lord thy God is with thee in all things whatsoever thou shalt go to." *

*   *   *

"God hath not given us the spirit of fear: but of power, and of love." **

*   *   *

Be It Done to You According to Your Faith. (Matt. ix. 29.)

---

* Josue i. 9.
** 2 Tim i. 7.

ARE YOU AWARE

of the power and beauty of the Mass? Are you interested in discussing it?

The following is a little talk which was presented by the collaborator, G. McL. H., to a group of non-Catholic friends:

I was asked to speak on the power and beauty of ritual. It occurred to me that discussion of the arts seldom brings light or understanding of their beauty or their power to move us.

After some thought I decided, that like the arts, the power and beauty of the ritual is most difficult to analyze. And I concluded that for this reason or perhaps because "Silence is Golden" they have been expressed, throughout the ages, by symbol and allegory.

The Mass, as everyone knows, is steeped in symbols which are expressed in terms of vestments, actions, music, incense, candles, altar, priest—all of which are highly significant—to mention a few symbols specifically.

The candles beautifully symbolize the mystery of light, the dispelling of darkness, the joy of the Lord, the Light of the world.

The vestments contain a mystical and a moral symbolism, mystically they represent Christ's passion. The virtue represented by each garment is recalled to the mind of the priest by the prayer which he says as he puts on the garments for the celebration of Mass. For example, as the priest puts on the alb (mystically the white garment in which Christ was clothed by Herod and his court) he prays, "Cleanse me. O Lord, and purify my heart, that being made white in the blood of the lamb, I may have fruition of everlasting joys."

The church is the sheepfold, the people the sheep, being fed by the priest, the apostle of Christ, with his arms outstretched representing Christ on His Cross—the covered chalice symbolizing the blindness of the Jews in not recognizing Christ as the Son of God and the Host—circular in form because the circle is the most perfect of figures. It is symbolic of infinity and is most appropriate to represent the presence of Him Who is infinite in love and Who offered a sacrifice of infinite merit. The bread and wine signify the Divine Victim as food for our souls and the union of the faithful in Christ, for as bread is made up of many grains and wine from numerous grapes, so the mystical body of Christ is formed from the multitude of the faithful. And it symbolizes the mortification which everyone must endure to be united with Christ; for as wheat must be ground and treated to be bread, so in like manner the individual soul to be united with Christ must die to itself. And hidden in the bread and wine is the mystery of faith—Christ mystically living on in His Church and in the souls of those who believe in Him.

At Mass we pray—"Let the sacred offering, O Lord, ever confer salutary benediction upon us, *perfecting in power what it doeth in symbol* through Christ our Lord."

The ritual of the Mass is a manifestation of reverence and worship of God: to acknowledge our dependence on Him, and is a means of offering ourselves to God through the merits of Jesus. The Mass is a public corporate prayer designed for a gathering consisting of different races and persons of every type of human culture. For this reason the ritual is objective, impartial, Catholic and yet at the same time it retains what can *satisfy* the needs and requirements of the soul—for the individual by his absorption into the higher unity finds liberty and discipline, group and solitary devotion.

The Mass is amazing in its completeness; its all inclusiveness. All the holy impatience and acts of the prophets find their accomplishment in the High Priest (which is Jesus) prefigured in the person of Aaron whom God Himself clothed with most magnificent vestment (Exod. xxviii. 29) and also in Melchisedech, who offered bread and wine to the Lord. (Gen. xiv. 18-20.) The prophecies are consummated; including that of Malachias who wrote, "For from the rising of the sun even to the going down; my name is great among the Gentiles, and in every place there is sacrifice; and there is offered in my name a clean oblation." (Mal. i. 11.) It is worthy of note that since the crucifixion there is no sacrifice in the Jewish ritual.

Perhaps another reason why the Mass is difficult to explain is that it is the drama of a sacred mystery and obviously a *mystery cannot be explained in such a way that there is no mystery left.* We believe that Jesus—in

His Sacred Humanity—is present on the altar under the appearance of bread and wine, because at the Last Supper Jesus said of the bread which He held in His hands—"This is My body." As Jesus was then living, the substance, the internal imperceptible element of bread by becoming His Body became His living self. We do not conclude this by our faculty of reason but on the testimony of Jesus. It is called the Mystery of Faith because the evidence for its truth is faith in the word of Christ Who declared—"This is My body, which is given for you." (Luke xxii. 19.)

I will present a few of the Mass prayers, although I fear that a summary, especially without the music, will not convey the spiritual power or the beauty of the Mass.

All the prayers are selected from the psalms, epistles and gospels. The celebrant, moving to different places and going up and down from the altar, symbolizes Jesus' journeying; His trials and resurrection, and it also symbolizes our journey and vicissitudes through life.

The Mass begins at the foot of the altar with the sign of the cross, the symbol of absolution, and the prayer—"I will go in to the altar of God, to God Who giveth joy to my youth.

"Send forth Thy light and Thy truth; they have conducted me and brought me unto Thy holy hill, and into 'Thy tabernacles.'" The confiteor is recited:

"Thou will turn again, O God, and quicken us. And Thy people will rejoice in Thee. O Lord, hear my prayer."

The priest says:

"The Lord be with you." And the people answer: "And with Thy Spirit." This aspiration is said seven times during the Mass.

Going up to the altar—

"Take away from us our iniquities, we beseech thee, O Lord; that, being made pure in heart we may be worthy to enter into the Holy of Holies, through Christ our Lord."

A great many of the prayers end with "Through Christ our Lord," because we are offering ourselves to God through the merits of Jesus.

THE INTROIT

"God Who sitteth in His holy place—God Who maketh them that are of one mind to dwell together in His house—He shall give strength and courage to His people."

The Kyrie Eleison

A cry for mercy—"Lord Have Mercy on Us."

And the Gloria—"Glory be to God on high; we bless Thee, we adore Thee, we glorify Thee. We give thanks for Thy great Glory. Who takest away the sins of the world *receive* our prayer."

The Offertory

At the Offertory our desire for union with Christ is expressed in the prayer: "O God, Who in creating man didst exalt his nature very wonderfully and yet more wonderfully didst establish it anew: grant that through the mystery of this water and wine we may be made partakers of His divinity who deigned to become partaker of our humanity."

The wine is offered "for our salvation and that of all mankind."

"I will compass Thy Altar—that I may hear the voice of praise—I have loved O Lord!

the beauty of Thy house and the place where Thy Glory dwelleth."

Now a prayer begins with words that tell us what our attitude should be.

"*Humbled in mind* and *contrite* of heart may we find favor with Thee O Lord; and may the sacrifice we this day offer up be well pleasing to Thee. Come, Thou, the Sanctifier; and bless this sacrifice which is prepared for the glory of Thy holy name."

"Receive, O Holy Trinity this oblation offered up by us to Thee in *memory* of the passion, resurrection and ascension of Our Lord, Jesus Christ, and in honor of the Blessed Mary; of John the Baptist, Peter, Paul and all the Saints that it may be available to their honor and to our salvation; and may they whose memory we celebrate on earth vouchsafe to intercede for us in heaven."

THE PREFACE

P. Ages throughout ages
The Lord be with you.

R. And with your spirit.

P. Lift up your hearts.

R. *We have them lifted up unto the Lord.*

P. Let us give thanks to the Lord our God.

R. It is meek and just.

AT THE SANCTUS

We believe the altar is surrounded by angels and we join them in singing—"Holy, Holy, Holy—the heavens and earth are full of Thy Glory."

"And do Thou, O God, vouchsafe in all respects to bless, consecrate and approve this our oblation, to *perfect* it, and render it well pleasing to Thyself so that it may become for us the body and blood of Thy most beloved Son Jesus our Lord.

We speak of the Sacrifice of the Mass because just as on the cross Jesus freely gave His Body to the executioners, thus offering Himself as a victim for atonement, so does He, at the Mass, freely put Himself in the hands of the priest to be offered up as a sacrifice for mankind.

At the Consecration Jesus speaks through the lips of the priest:

"Take ye and eat ye all of this. For this is My Body. And drink ye all of this. For this is the Chalice of My Blood, of the new and everlasting testament (the mystery of faith), which for you and many shall be shed unto the remission of sins."

"As often as ye shall do these things, ye shall do them in memory of me."

There are several prayers in which we ask the Lord to look upon our oblation "with a gracious and tranquil countenance" and to accept them as He did the sacrifice of Abel, Abraham and "that which Thy Priest Melchisedech offered up to Thee, 'a holy sacrifice, a victim without blemish.' "

And we humbly pray that they "be borne by the hands of Thy Holy Angel to Thine Altar on high in the Presence of Thy Divine Majesty." And that as many "as shall receive the most sacred Body and Blood of Thy Son—shall be filled with every heavenly blessing and grace."

The action of the Mass goes beyond time and space; it reaches to eternity and recalls the fellowship of man.

We pray for all "who have gone before

us." And we pray—may "Thy servants who put our trust in the multitudes of Thy mercy vouchsafe to grant some part and fellowship with Thy apostles, martyrs and saints. *Into their company do Thou we beseech Thee admit us,* not weighing our merits but freely pardoning our offenses." Through Christ our Lord "by whom Thou dost always create, sanctify, quicken, bless, and bestow upon us all, these good things."

This is followed by the Lord's Prayer, and prayers asking that we be delivered from all evil "past, present and to come"—a prayer for peace "in our day"—a prayer for mercy —a plea for the cooperation of the Holy Spirit to help us "cleave to Thy commandments and never suffer me to be separated from Thee."

"May this communion, through Thy loving kindness be to me a safeguard and remedy for soul and body who with God the Father in the unity of the Holy Ghost liveth and reignest God—ages throughout ages."

At the Communion

The Host is raised symbolizing Christ raised on His cross.

"What shall I render unto the Lord for all the things that He hath rendered unto me? I will take the Chalice of salvation and will call upon the name of the Lord. With high praises will I call upon the Lord, and I shall be saved from all my enemies."

All the post-Communion prayers are very ancient.

"Bestow Thy plenteous gifts on our senses, O Almighty God. And through the temporal death of Thy Son of which the august mysteries give testimony we may have confidence that Thou hast given us life everlasting." (Wednesday in Holy Week.)

The Priest's Blessing

May Almighty God the Father and the Son and the Holy Ghost bless you.

The Mass ends with the first chapter of the Gospel of St. John. It is a summary of all the benefits which we receive through the sacrifice of Christ. And it reminds us that, at

Mass, we are endeavoring to let God become "The Word" in us.

"In the beginning was the Word—and the Word was God—and the Word was with God —He came unto His own—*But as many as received Him to them He gave power to become the sons of God*—And the Word was made flesh; and dwelt among us full of grace and truth—and we saw His glory."

One Sunday when I was at Mass I saw the West Point Cadets walk up the aisle with their heads bowed and hands clasped in prayer.

They filled the sanctuary and choir loft. As they chanted the prayers, I thought: this is indeed beautiful. It was very evident that they had powerfully affected the minds and hearts of the congregation—surely a symbol of beauty and power.

It occurred to me that perhaps many Catholics have little conscious recognition, or interest, in symbols; that they know *well* how to adore God and cherish their faith: but have little concern for arguing or explaining it; they love the beauty of their Father's house and delight in going to the place "where His

Glory dwelleth" — there to worship in His Majestic Presence without, perhaps, being consciously aware of the divine realities, truth, mysteries and symbols in which their souls live. But—

"Kneeling, breathless, in the holy place
We know immortal beauty face to face."

"DEARLY BELOVED, CONCERN-
ING ALL THINGS I MAKE IT MY
PRAYER THAT THOU MAYEST
PROCEED PROSPEROUSLY, AND
FARE WELL . . ."

(3 John i. 2.)

NOTE

THE Holy Catholic Church was left by Jesus as the official custodian of all His Teachings, therefore of all sound Doctrine.

Religious groups usually owe their existence to the special emphasis placed by them upon one or more than one of Jesus' teachings. For instance, certain Religious groups bring into prominence The Virtue of Faith; others, Devotion to the Holy Spirit; others, Abandonment to the Divine Will. And these are, of course, Catholic Doctrines. This pamphlet contains Catholic teaching concerning Doctrines which are specially emphasized by certain Religious groups and in addition stresses others closely allied.

The method used in presenting these Doctrines presupposes that those reading the pamphlet have already been taught Catholic principles in a logical manner.

However, at different periods, the needs of life require that particular Doctrines be reconsidered in the light of their application to daily living.

This pamphlet is a psychological challenge to the reader to consider his own personal application of the Truths presented, especially the fundamental Catholic Doctrine concerning The Divine Indwelling in Souls possessing Sanctifying Grace.

The Biblical texts used in the pamphlet have been taken either from the Douay, or Westminster translations of Holy Scripture.

SUGGESTED READING

The Holy Bible.

Self-Knowledge and Self-Discipline, Rev. B. W. Maturin, St. Anthony Guild Press, Paterson, N. J.

God Within Us—and other books, by Rev. Raoul Plus, S.J., P. J. Kenedy & Sons, 12 Barclay Street, New York, N. Y.

Progress Through Mental Prayer; The Holy Ghost, Rev. Edward Leen, C.S.Sp., Sheed & Ward, New York, N. Y.

Think and Pray; A Primer of Prayer (Longmans, Green & Co., New York), *The Sacrament of Duty* (P. J. Kenedy & Sons, New York), *Devotion to the Holy Spirit* (pamphlet) (The Paulist Press, 401 West 59th Street, New York), all by Rev. Joseph McSorley, C.S.P.

An Easy Method of Mental Prayer (pamphlet), Rev. Bertrand Wilberforce, O.P., International Catholic Truth Society.

Come Holy Ghost (pamphlet), Rev. R. F. Clarke, S.J., International Catholic Truth Society.

Contemplation of Christ, St. Augustine, Catholic Truth Society, 407 Bergen Street, Brooklyn, N. Y.

How to Pray, Abbé Grou, Benziger Brothers, 26 Park Place, New York, N. Y.

The Practice of the Presence of God, Brother Lawrence of the Resurrection, Benziger Brothers, 26 Park Place, New York, N. Y.

The Cenacle (50 Meditations on The Holy Spirit Collected in 1696), Carmelite Convent, Boston, Mass.

The Internal Mission of the Holy Ghost, Cardinal H. E. Manning, P. J. Kenedy & Sons, 12 Barclay Street, New York, N. Y.

Christ the Life of the Soul, Dom Columba Marmion, O.S.B., B. Herder Book Company, St. Louis, Mo.

The Indwelling of the Holy Spirit, Barthelemy Froget, O.P., The Paulist Press, 401 West 59th Street, New York, N. Y.

The Summa—Parts One and Two, St. Thomas Aquinas, Benziger Brothers, 26 Park Place, New York, N. Y.

A Companion to the Summa—Volume II, Rev. Walter Farrell, O.P., S.T.Lr., S.T.D., Sheed & Ward, New York, N. Y.

The Way of Simplicity, Rev. William E. Orchard, D.D., Sheed & Ward, New York, N. Y.

The Temple (A Book of Prayer), Rev. William E. Orchard, D.D., E. P. Dutton & Co., Inc., 286-302 Fourth Avenue, New York, N. Y.

God and Intelligence; Religion Without God, Monsignor Fulton J. Sheen, Longmans, Green & Co., New York, N. Y.

The Long Road Home, John Moody, Macmillian Co., New York, N. Y.

"THE KINGDOM OF GOD
(Life, Truth, Love, Goodness, Wisdom)

is within

YOU."

SEEK IT—FIND IT—USE IT.

CPSIA information can be obtained
at www.ICGtesting.com
Printed in the USA
FSHW011955050820
72685FS